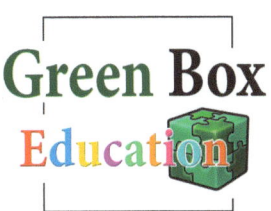

Green Box Kids Learn About Sharing

A comic book-based social skills curriculum

Written by:
Carl Dzyak, M.Ed., BCBA, LBA
Barbara Kaminski, Ph.D., BCBA-D, LBA
Christopher Richardson, M.Ed., BCBA, LBA

Illustrated by:
Sarah Miller

Copyright ©2016 Green Box ABA, PLLC
All Rights Reserved by, and remain the intellectual property of, the Author.

This book is for individual or classroom use only. This product contains copyrighted text and graphics. Except as permitted under the Copyright Act of 1976, no part of this book may be reproduced in any form or by any electronic or mechanical means, including the use of information storage and retrieval systems, without permission in writing from the copyright owner. Requests for permissions should be addressed in writing to Green Box ABA, PLLC, Attn: Carl Dzyak, 6216 Old Keene Mill Court, Springfield, VA 22152

This is a work of fiction. Names, characters, businesses, places, events and incidents are either the products of the author's imagination or used in a fictitious manner. Any resemblance to actual persons, living or dead, or actual events is purely coincidental.

This book is not intended as a substitute for the medical advice of physicians. The reader should regularly consult a physician in matters relating to his/her health and particularly with respect to any symptoms that may require diagnosis or medical attention.

www.greenboxABA.org

www.facebook.com/GreenBoxABA

www.twitter.com/GreenBoxEdu

This book is dedicated to the cool kids who do the awesome things that inspire us every day.

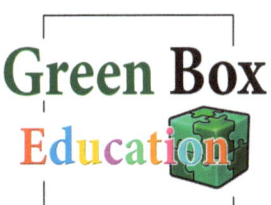

Table of Contents

Welcome to the Green Box Social Skills Curriculum!...........1
   Social Skills Are Foundational!...........1
   What Is Applied Behavior Analysis?...........2
   Overview of The Green Box Kids Social Skills Curriculum...........2
   About This Volume...........4
   How To Use This Book...........4
   How To Measure Progress...........5
   Summary and Extension...........6

Lesson 1: The Soccer Game...........7
   Let's Break It Down!...........10
   Let's Think About It!...........17
   Let's See What We Learned!...........25
   Let's See What The Green Box Kids Came Up With!...........28

Lesson 2: The Video Game...........31
   Let's Break It Down!...........34
   Let's Think About It!...........41
   Let's See What We Learned!...........47
   Let's See What The Green Box Kids Came Up With!...........50

Lesson 3: Homework...........53
   Let's Break It Down!...........56
   Let's Think About It...........63
   Let's See What We Learned!...........70
   Let's See What The Green Box Kids Came Up With!...........73

Appendix A: Measuring Progress...........77
Appendix B: Individualized Education Program Goals...........83
Appendix C: For the ABA Professional...........85

Introduction

Welcome To The Green Box Social Skills Curriculum!

Each volume of the curriculum concentrates on a specific social skill that may present a challenge, particularly for a child with special needs. Each of the three lessons in every volume consists of a comic and activities. The comics feature the Green Box Kids in challenging social scenarios. The interactions are presented with minimal text in a child-friendly, visually-striking format to help engage the student in the social lesson with ease and enjoyment.

Social Skills Are Foundational!

Family. School. Neighborhoods. Sports Teams. Clubs. The enjoyment and success of participating in such social groups is related, in many ways, to the ability to function in social settings. Given the amount of time spent in social groups, both as a child and into adulthood, learning social skills is a vital component of a child's overall development.

Social Skills Impairments in Children with Special Needs

While all children sometimes experience difficulties navigating complicated social situations, the child with special needs often needs extra help and support. Research has shown social skills impairments in children diagnosed with conduct disorders, mood disorders, anxiety disorders, autism spectrum disorders, attention-deficit/hyperactivity disorder (ADHD), learning disabilities, and other behavioral challenges (Rutherford et al., 2004).

Typical deficits include difficulty initiating and responding in social interactions, making and maintaining eye contact, reading non-verbal cues (including facial expressions and body language), taking another person's perspective, recognizing feelings, and knowing what to talk about and for how long.

Consequences of Social Skills Impairments

When supported learning opportunities are not provided, the lack of positive peer interactions can lead to avoidance of social opportunities and a downward spiral, as fewer opportunities for learning are encountered. This makes it difficult for a child to develop and maintain meaningful personal relationships. Often, as a result, these children gravitate towards solitary play and activities.

Teaching Social Skills

Finding ways and opportunities to practice social interaction skills in a supportive environment can be difficult. However, while not as straightforward to teach as, for example, multiplication facts, social skills _can_ be taught and strengthened. Children with special learning needs may require intentional instruction that can include modeling, role playing social scenarios, social stories, and instruction based on the techniques and principles of Applied Behavior Analysis.

What Is Applied Behavior Analysis?

Conceptual Foundation

Based on learning theory (Skinner, 1953), Applied Behavior Analysis (ABA) is a scientific approach for teaching new skills and decreasing behaviors that are harmful or interfere with learning.

Because of its scientific foundation, ABA focuses on measurable behavior change that is the result of events that occur before and/or after a behavior (Baer et al, 1968). Events that occur after a behavior and increase its likelihood of reoccurring are called reinforcers. On the other hand, punishment after a behavior decreases the likelihood it will occur again.

Teaching Strategies

ABA Practitioners (Board Certified Behavior Analysts or BCBAs) use many different teaching strategies. These include specific instructional techniques, such as direct instruction and discrete trial training. "Shaping," the process of teaching closer and closer approximations to the desired skill, is a commonly used technique. Another is "chaining," in which smaller skills are learned and linked together to accomplish a larger task.

However, ABA is not a "one size fits all" approach; because the needs for each child are different, the goals and strategies used to achieve them are individually tailored for each child. Progress is continuously measured and modifications to goals and strategies are based on the measured outcomes, resulting in efficient and effective treatment.

Goals

ABA has been used to help improve the lives of individuals by focusing on behaviors that are socially significant for the individual. A wide variety of different skills, such as communication & language skills, academics, self-help skills, work skills, domestic and life skills, self-monitoring, play skills, and social skills have been taught using ABA strategies. ABA principles have also been used to help decrease problematic behaviors, such as self-injury and aggression. In all cases, the goal is to bring about meaningful and positive behavior change.

Overview of the Green Box Kids Social Skills Curriculum

Developed by a team of BCBAs and professional artists, the Green Box Kids Social Skills Curriculum and supplemental materials support a comprehensive approach to social skills training. Although the curriculum evolved from application of principles of behavior analysis, no special training in ABA is necessary to use the materials. Our mission is to provide professionals, including speech and language pathologists, special educators, psychologists, counselors, and applied behavior analysts with engaging tools that are inherently motivating for learners. Additionally, we aim to provide parents with the tools they need to address social skills challenges, even if they cannot access private therapy on their own.

Relatable Characters

The Green Box Kids Social Skills Curriculum offers a unique approach to social skills lessons by introducing relatable characters that are easy for children to connect with. The Green Box Kids are a group of elementary school-aged friends who deal with the kinds of social skills challenges that many students regularly encounter. Each of the kids has

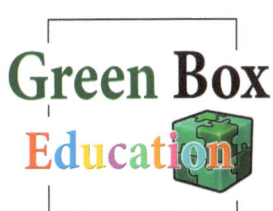

unique likes, dislikes, strengths, and challenges that define them. As learners get to know each character, they may find themselves relating to their favorite Green Box Kids' quirks and idiosyncrasies. Just like regular kids, the Green Box Kids are not perfect.

Realistic Scenarios in Comic Book Format

The art in the Green Box Kids curriculum is presented in a comic book format. Unlike other popular materials, the lessons contain minimal text, which allows learners to easily navigate social lessons without being burdened with unnecessary language. Because the kids look and act like real kids participating in real life scenarios, students have the opportunity to observe and reflect on realistic facial expressions and body language, which are critical building blocks to social development.

Active Responding and Practice

Through active responding and practice, the activities in the book create opportunities for new skills to be acquired and strengthened in a supported environment that promotes successful social interactions. Real world social interactions are often complex, unpredictable, and varied. To reflect this, an answer key is not included for these activities, leaving flexibility for answers based on the varied, but appropriate, ways to react to a social situation.

Meet the Kids! Cami, Mei, Lucy, Tito, Barry, Richard, Jack, and Lisa

About This Volume

Sharing

In each of the three social comics and lessons in this volume, the Green Box Kids learn more about what it means to **share** and why it is important. Sharing is a vital life and social skill that children need to learn in order to make and keep friends and in a social setting, such as a classroom. While sharing can be a challenge, it can be learned and developed with practice and support.

When we share with others, we give them all or a part of something that we have. The lessons in this volume help children learn how to ask appropriately to share, what to do when someone does not want to or cannot share, what to do when you don't want to share, and whether something is appropriate to share. For example, Lesson 1 leads the learner through a scenario in which it would be inappropriate to share (a water bottle). Importantly, the comics show the reactions of all of the people involved in the social interaction to show how the actions of each Green Box Kids affects their friendships. The supporting activities walk your learner though the concept of sharing as they compare what they are learning to what happens to their favorite Green Box Kids characters.

How To Use This Book

The Green Box Kids Social Skills Curriculum is ideally used in a group setting with similar-aged peers and/or other children at a comparable developmental level. Group settings provide opportunities for discussion, sharing of ideas and real-life scenarios, and active practice of the skills. However, the materials can be used individually, for example, in the home, with the parent filling the role of the social "peer."

Each lesson focuses on a different component of the social skill. However, all of the lessons are set-up in the same format. Each lesson consists of:

Warm-Up Questions

Each lesson starts with a series of "warm-up" questions about the topic. Use these questions to find out how much the learner already knows about the topic that will be covered. These questions introduce the topic and will be answered in the course of the lesson, so you don't need to spend too much time discussing them.

The Comic

In 6 – 7 panels, the comic sets up a socially-based problem and an "inappropriate" solution to the problem.

Breakdown of Comic, Panel By Panel

The comic is broken down, panel by panel, with 1 – 2 questions that encourage the learner to concentrate on social cues (facial expressions, body language) for clues. This facilitates conversation about and engagement with the characters' feelings and reactions.

Follow-up Questions

A series of follow-up questions are included to check comprehension of the events and concepts presented in the comic.

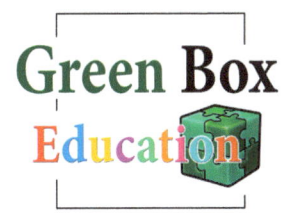

Learning Activities

Two to three learning activities, presented in a variety of learning formats, provide practice with the social concepts. Many of the activities are designed to be completed with a partner or group, opening the door for application and practice of the skill.

Solution Comic & Wrap-up Discussion

Each lesson ends with an opportunity for the learner to draw a comic panel with a guess about a solution to the social problem. An appropriate solution comic is then presented, along with 1 or 2 questions designed to wrap-up the lesson. You may also go back and ask the Warm-up Questions again to see how much the student has learned.

Tips

- Use social praise for appropriate responses and interactions.
- Although space has been provided for written answers, learners may either write in their own answers or give them verbally, depending on skill level.
- If used in a group, as the adult you should be sure to function as a discussion leader
    - Encourage the group to go beyond just answering the question and to "dig deeper"
    - During the discussion, relate the answers to real-life examples
    - Don't let the discussion get off-topic
    - Don't let one or two kids dominate the discussion
    - Find ways to involve everyone in the group discussion and activities
- Provide guidance and prompts/suggestions, as needed. But encourage peer facilitation.
- Whenever possible, find ways during the lessons to provide opportunities to practice the skill in the social group setting.

How To Measure Progress

Measuring progress is an essential component of any curriculum. Below is guidance for measuring progress. For parents or educators with little to no experience in Applied Behavior Analysis (ABA), we have included a straightforward and easy way to measure development of skills (Appendix A). Progress in the school setting can be measured by including a sharing goal on the child's Individualized Education Program (IEP). Some suggested IEP goals can be found in Appendix B. For ABA professionals and educators with more experience in ABA, a more detailed behavior change program is outlined in Appendix C.

Let's say that you want to know if a child is making progress in learning math facts. A common assessment method is the "speed drill," in which the child is given one minute to complete a worksheet with one hundred math problems. It is not unusual to administer a speed drill before any instruction begins (a "pretest", in order to determine how much the child already knows. The speed drill may be given weekly, until the child receives a particular score (for example, at least 90 correct out of 100).

Measuring progress made while learning social skills is a bit more complex but conceptually the same. There are two things that you will need to decide: (1) what to measure and (2) when to measure.

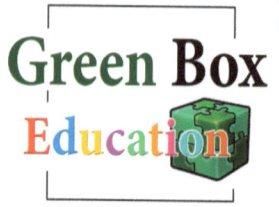

What to Measure

Progress should be shown not only in how a learner answers the questions in this book but also in development of overall skills. We recommend using the materials found in Appendix A to assess overall skill development. The rating scale and checklist help determine how much the child has learned about how to ask appropriately to share, what to do when someone does not want to or cannot share, what to do when you don't want to share, and whether something is appropriate to share.

When to Measure

As with the speed drills, it is best to first determine what the child already knows or can do. Therefore, we recommend assessing the current skill level before you begin using the materials. Then, after the book has been completed, assess how much the child has learned. Because each of the lessons in this book focus on a different component of the social skill, you could do a learning check after each lesson, similar to administering speed drills once a week.

Summary and Extension

After this book has been completed, the learner should have a greater understanding of the targeted social skill and the ways in which it is important for developing and maintaining relationships with others. Additionally, the child will have learned some strategies related to displaying the skill. However, social skill development is a process and you should continue to provide opportunities for practice. Children who are still developing foundational social skills often feel more comfortable in small groups. Regardless of the group size, try to make the environment comfortable and supportive, while providing feedback, guidance, and praise for appropriate behaviors. Finally, don't forget that adult behavior can provide a good example of how to respond to social situations, so find and use opportunities to model appropriate responses.

References

Baer, D.M., Wolf, M.M., & Risley, T.R., (1968). Some current dimensions of applied behavior analysis. *Journal of Applied Behavior Analysis,* 1, 91-97.

Rutherford, R.B.Jr., Quinn, M.M., & Mathur, S.R. (2004). Handbook of Research in Emotional and Behavioral Disorders. New York, NY: The Guilford Press.

Skinner, B.F. (1953). Science and Human Behavior. New York, NY: The MacMillian Press.

Let's Learn About Sharing
Lesson 1: The Soccer Game

Find out what you already know about sharing.

1. What is sharing?
_____
_____
_____

2. Think of a time someone did not share with you. How did it make you feel?
_____
_____
_____

3. Think of a time someone did share with you. How did it make you feel?
_____
_____
_____

4. Does sharing help you make new friends? Why or why not?
_____
_____
_____

5. Your family has a new trampoline. You got home from school, grabbed a quick snack, and headed straight out to the trampoline. Your brother stayed after school and got home later. Now, that he is home, he would like to jump on the trampoline. What should you and your brother do?
_____
_____
_____

Lesson 1: The Soccer Game

Read the comic on the following page about Tito and Lucy to learn about a time when sharing did not go so well. Make sure to look closely at the faces to see how they may be feeling.

Let's Break it Down!

Now we are going to break the comic down to get a better idea of what is going on in each picture.

What's happening in this picture?

What is Lucy doing here?

Look at Tito's face and body language. How does he feel?

What does Tito's face tell you about how he feels?

What does Lucy's face tell you about what she is thinking?

What is happening in this picture?

Let's Think About It.

The questions on the following page will help us better understand the comic we just read.

Answer the following questions about the comic you just read. Some questions may have more than one right answer.

1. How would you have responded to Tito if you were Lucy?
   _____
   _____
   _____

2. What cues does Tito give that tell Lucy he is thirsty?
   _____
   _____
   _____

3. In this scenario, is it okay to not share? Why or why not?
   _____
   _____
   _____

4. Should Lucy have shared her water with Tito?
   _____
   _____
   _____

5. Who could the kids ask for help in this situation?
   _____
   _____
   _____

6. How did Lucy feel at the end of the comic?
_____
_____
_____

7. How do you think Lucy would have felt if she had forgotten her water?
_____
_____
_____

8. How could Lucy still help Tito if she decides it would not be a good idea to share her water?
_____
_____
_____

9. How did Tito feel at the end of the comic?
_____
_____
_____

10. Was Lucy's behavior polite?
_____
_____
_____

Should I Share?

In this next section we will look at some times when sharing might *not* be the best option. The rules about sharing are not always black and white; sometimes there are gray areas.

Talk about it with your friends!

Do we have to share every time someone asks?

Should other people share with me every time I ask?

What do you do if...?

1. What do you do if someone asks you to share your lunch and your school has a "No sharing food or drink" policy?

_____
_____
_____
_____

2. What do you do if a stranger tries to share candy with you?

_____
_____
_____
_____

3. What do you do if someone asks you to share personal information like your address? How can you tell if the person is safe?

_____
_____
_____
_____

4. What do you do if you just got a brand new game and your friend tells you that, "If you don't let me borrow that game tonight, then I'm going to tell the teacher that you're bad at sharing!"

_____
_____
_____
_____

5. What do you do if someone asks if they can share drugs or alcohol with you?
_____
_____
_____
_____

6. What do you do if a friend tries to share a toy with you and you do not want to play with it?
_____
_____
_____
_____

Hmm, what about a water bottle?

Use the Venn Diagram below to help you come up with a list of:

- Things that are **Always** a good idea to share.

- Things that are **Never** a good idea to share.

- Things that are in that "gray area" we talked about earlier.

Use the table below to make lists for "Sharing Rules."

Things we should always share.	Things we should ask adults about before sharing.	Things we should not share.

Let's See What We Learned!

Let's go back to the original comic. Look it over one more time and come up with an idea for what you think Lucy should do.

What do you think should happen next?

Draw what you think Lucy should do:

Let's See What The Green Box Kids Came Up With!

Lisa knows that Tito also needs water and offers to help him find some.

Talk with your friends about their solutions.

Let's Learn About Sharing Lesson 2: The Video Game

Find out what you already know about sharing.

1. Do you need to share every time someone asks?
___
___
___

2. How can you ask a friend to share?
___
___
___

3. How do you know if someone wants you to share?
___
___
___

4. What are some times when it is best not to share?
___
___
___

5. What is something that you can share that you can't hold in your hand?
___
___
___

Lesson 2: The Video Game

Read the comic on the following page about Barry and Richard to learn about a time when sharing did not go so well. Make sure to look closely at the Green Box Kids' faces to see how they may be feeling.

Let's Break It Down!

Now we are going to break the comic down to get a better idea of what is going on in each picture.

What are Richard and Barry doing?

Why is Richard telling Barry to "watch out"?

What is Richard really trying to say?

Look at Richard's face. How is he feeling?

What does Barry's face and body language tell you about how he is feeling?

39

What is Richard's facial expression?

Let's Think About It.

The questions on the following page will help us better understand the comic we just read.

Answer the following questions about the comic you just read. Some questions may have more than one right answer.

1. What was the problem with sharing in this comic?
_____
_____
_____

2. Did Richard want Barry to share and how do you know?
_____
_____
_____

3. Does Barry want to share? How do you know?
_____
_____
_____

4. Did Barry notice how Richard was feeling?
_____
_____
_____

5. How does Richard feel at the end of the story?
_____
_____
_____

6. Did Richard ever tell Barry that he wanted a turn on the game?
___
___
___

7. What are different ways to handle when someone will not share with you?
___
___
___

8. Did Richard and Barry find a fair way to share the video game? If not, how could they?
___
___
___

9. Is there a way to play a one player game with two people?
___
___
___

10. What could Richard have done differently to let Barry know that he would like to play?
___
___
___

I Want It. You Want It. Who Gets It?

Let's face it. Sometimes sharing is hard. If you have something or are doing something that you really like (like Barry and the video game), it can be hard to give someone else a turn – or even notice that they want one. In the next section we will talk about how we still share.

Talk about it with your friends!

Think about a time a friend didn't want to share with you and talk about it with your friends.

Think about a time that you didn't want to share and talk about it with your friends.

For each problem, figure out a solution where only you get what you want (I want it), only your friend gets what they want (You want it), and a way you can share.

	I Want it	You Want it	Let's Share
There is only one cookie left.			
You are playing with your new water blaster. Your friend wants to play with it, too.			
Your brother is building with Legos®. Legos® are your favorite toy.			

Circle some things that are OK to share with friends.

What is something you **do not** like to share with friends?
_____
_____
_____

If your friend wants to play with something you don't want to share, what can you do?
_____
_____
_____

Let's See What We Learned!

Let's go back to the original comic. Look it over one more time and come up with an idea for what you think the Green Box Kids should do.

What do you think should happen next?

Draw what you think the Kids should do:

Let's See What The Green Box Kids Came Up With!

Barry lets Richard have a turn.

Talk with your friends about their solution.

Let's Learn About Sharing Lesson 3: Homework

Find out what you already know about sharing.

1. Is it hard to share things you really like? Explain.
   _____
   _____
   _____

2. Do you like to spend time with friends who share?
   _____
   _____
   _____

3. What about people who never share – do you like spending time with them?
   _____
   _____
   _____

4. Is there a difference between asking to share something you really need and something you just really like?
   _____
   _____
   _____

5. You forgot the instructions for a special project at school. You ask a friend if you can borrow them and he says, "No, I am using them." What could you do?
   _____
   _____
   _____

Lesson 3: Homework

Read the comic on the following page about Jack and Lisa to learn about a time when sharing did not go so well. Make sure to look closely at the Green Box Kids' faces to see how they may be feeling.

Let's Break It Down!

Now we are going to break the comic down to get a better idea of what is going on in each picture.

What are Lisa and Jack focusing on?

What happened in this picture?

How is Lisa feeling? How can you tell?

Talk about Jack's facial expression.

What's happening in this picture?

Look at Lisa's face. How is she feeling?

Let's Think About It.

The questions on the following page will help us better understand the comic we just read.

Answer the following questions about the comic you just read. Some questions may have more than one right answer.

1. Do you think Jack's response to Lisa was helpful? Why or why not?
___
___
___

2. Are school supplies a good thing to share?
___
___
___

3. Could Jack have done anything to help Lisa if he did not want to share his pencil sharpener?
___
___
___

4. Why do you think Jack did not want to share the pencil sharpener?
___
___
___

5. Why is Jack concerned about finishing his work before dark?
___
___
___

6. Is there any advice you could give Jack to encourage him to share his school supplies?
___
___
___

7. What is something you could do when a friend or classmate does not want to share with you?
___
___
___

8. Did Lisa get angry with Jack? How did she feel?
___
___
___

9. What are some polite ways to ask for help at home or in school?
___
___
___

10. Are there things Lisa could have said to convince Jack to let her share the pencil sharpener?
___
___
___

Sharing is Caring.

Sharing is something we can do to show our friends and family that we care about them. And it can help us make new friends.

Talk about it with your friends!

How does it make you feel when a friend shares something you want or need?

If you share with a friend, do you think they will want to share back with you?

Lisa is trying to finish her homework, but now her pencil is broken and Jack isn't letting her use his pencil sharpener! Use red and green markers or colored pencils to fill in the circle next to each suggestion to show if that's a good idea 🟢 or a bad idea 🔴.

○ Since Jack won't share with Lisa, Lisa should grab the pencil sharpener from Jack and use it anyway!

○ Lisa should go and ask an adult if they have a pencil sharpener.

○ Lisa should go and quietly look for another pencil.

○ Lisa should tell Jack that he's a bad friend for not sharing.

○ Lisa should look and see if he has another pen or pencil.

○ Lisa should take Jack's pencil.

○ Lisa should tell Jack that she is upset and worried about the homework, then ask him again if she could use Jack's pencil sharpener.

○ Lisa should look around the room and see if there is another pencil sharpener she could use.

Sometimes sharing is hard, but having someone not want to share with you is hard too!

Write about a time when you didn't want to share with someone:

_____
_____
_____
_____
_____
_____

Did they get mad at you for not sharing with them?

_____

Write a way that you could have shared something else with them that would have made you both happy:

_____
_____
_____
_____
_____

Don't Get Mad

Sometimes our friends don't want to share and that can make us feel frustrated or mad. Or a friend might act angry if you don't want to share right now. If a friend yells or uses mean words, how does that make you feel? _____

_____

With a partner, think of some things you can say or do and some things that you should not say or do when sharing is hard.

Do	Don't
_____	_____
_____	_____
_____	_____
_____	_____
_____	_____

Let's See What We Learned!

Let's go back to the original comic. Look it over one more time and come up with an idea for what you think the Green Box Kids should do.

What do you think should happen next?

Draw what you think the Kids should do:

Let's See What The Green Box Kids Came Up With!

Jack lets Lisa use the pencil sharpener.

Talk with your friends about their solution.

Appendix A: Measuring Progress

Sharing Pre-Test

Before you begin using the lessons, use this pre-test to determine the child's current skill level.

The scales below describe different kinds of sharing scenarios. Rate HOW OFTEN the child engages in each behavior without any adult assistance. Base your ratings on recent observations.

Shares only appropriate items/activities (*Shares items that are appropriate to share and does not share when inappropriate*):

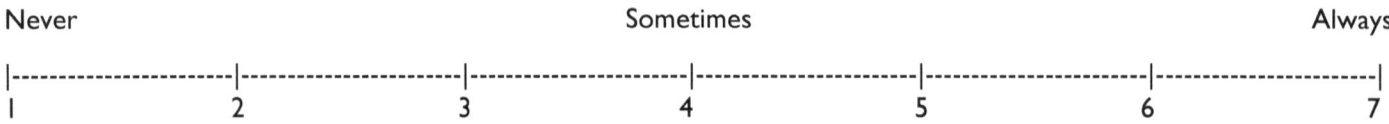

Asks to share appropriately (*Uses calm and appropriate language*):

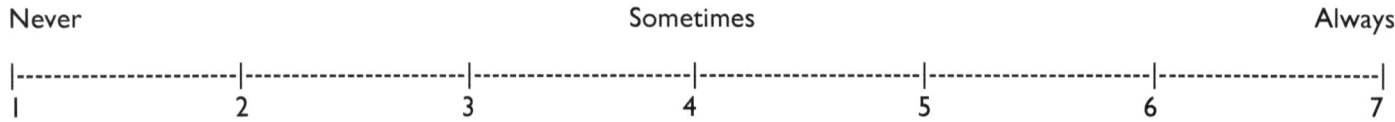

Gives an appropriate response when a sharing request is denied (*Suggests compromise, accepts denial, etc.*):

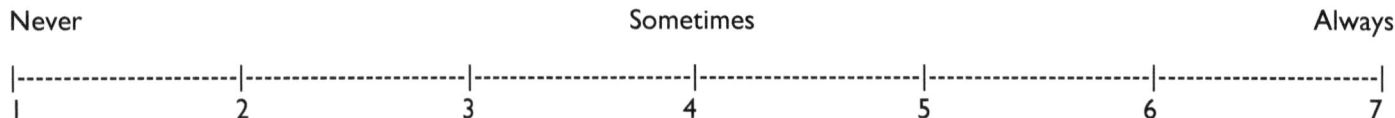

Honors sharing requests appropriately (*Hands over, rather than throws item, etc*):

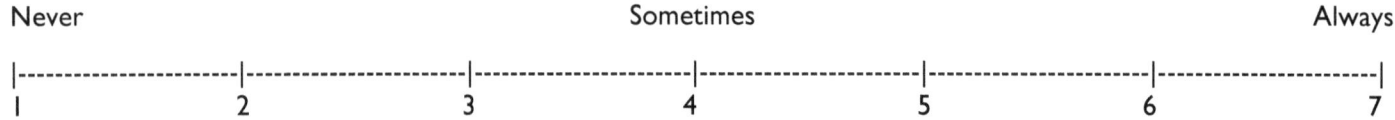

Denies sharing requests appropriately (*When denying a request, does so appropriately suggests an alternative, does not taunt, etc*):

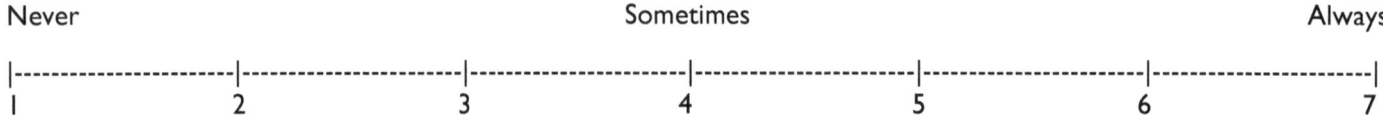

Sharing Behavior Checklist

After you have completed the pretest, use this form to track development of sharing skills while using the lessons.

Instructions:

- Whenever you notice the child engaging in a sharing opportunity use the form on the next page to:
    - Record the date.
    - Make notes about the activity. This could include the setting, who is present and/or how many other children are present, as well as what activities they are engaged in.
    - In the Skill section, make a checkmark in the box that most accurately describes the skill being displayed (note that these are also the skills assessed in the pretest).
    - In the Child's Response section, make a checkmark in the box that most accurately describe the way that the child responded.
        - Independently: Responded correctly without any adult assistance
        - Prompted: Responded correctly with adult assistance
        - Did not occur: A correct response did not occur
        - Problem Behavior: Some problem behavior occurred in response (tantrums when sharing request is denied, etc.)

Where to track skills:

- If you are using the lessons in a group format, use the form on the following page to track skills displayed in that setting.
- Other settings in which you can track skills:
    - Classroom
    - Home
    - Social groups (scout meetings, teams, clubs, etc.)

Measuring Progress:

- The goal is for the child to respond more frequently without adult assistance.
- If you are working with an ABA or other professional, you can share this information with them.

Extension:

You may continue to track the development of sharing skills after you have completed the lessons using this form.

Sharing Behavior Checklist

Date	Activity	Skill (check one)					Child's Response (check one)			
		Shares only appropriate items/activities	Asks to share appropriately	Gives an appropriate response when a sharing request is denied	Honors sharing requests appropriately	Denies sharing requests appropriately	Independently	Prompted	Did not Occur	Problem Behavior

Sharing Post-Test

After finishing the lessons, use this post-test to determine the child's current skill level. DO NOT REVIEW THE PRE-TEST SCORES!

The scales below describe different kinds of sharing scenarios. Rate HOW OFTEN the child engages in each behavior without any adult assistance. Base your ratings on current behavior only.

Shares only appropriate items/activities (*Shares items that are appropriate to share and does not share when inappropriate*):

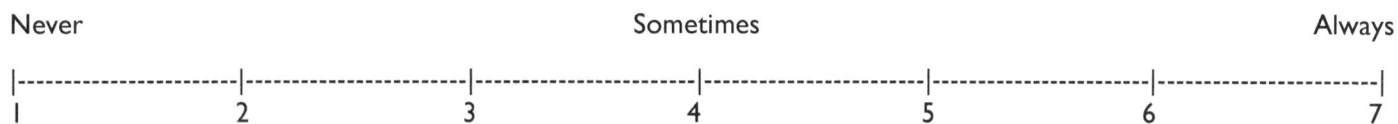

Asks to share appropriately (*Uses calm and appropriate language*):

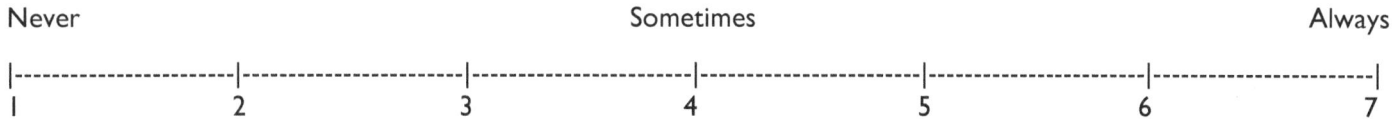

Gives an appropriate response when a sharing request is denied (*Suggests compromise, accepts denial, etc.*):

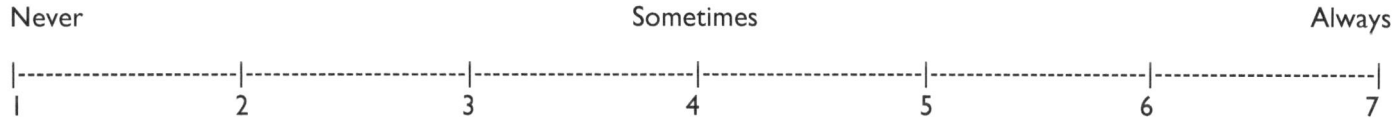

Honors sharing requests appropriately (*Hands over, rather than throws item, etc*):

Denies sharing requests appropriately (*When denying a request, does so appropriately suggests an alternative, does not taunt, etc*):

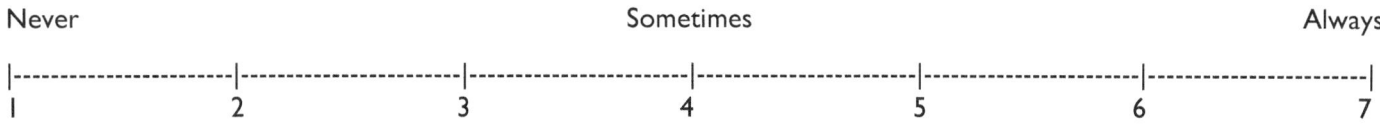

Pre-Post Comparison

- Fill in the chart below to compare sharing skills before and after using the lessons.

- To determine the degree of change (Change Score), subtract the pre-test score from the post-test score.

- For each item on the scale, more appropriate responses receive higher valued scores. Any change scores that are greater than 1, indicate that you have seen a change in that skill.

- Any skills that were scored lower on the Post-Test than the Pre-Test may need additional training. However, it is also possible that after using both the lessons and Sharing Checklist you are a more keen observer than before. This increased awareness to the types of responses the child is making may account for lower scores.
    - Compare the progress on the Sharing Checklist with the scores.
        - If the child is showing progress (more independent responses) on the Checklist, then progress is being made.
        - If the child is not showing progress on the Checklist, then additional learning opportunities and direct teaching is needed.

Skill	Pre-Test Score	Post-Test Score	Change (Post-test minus Pre-test) Score
Shares only appropriate items/activities			
Asks to share appropriately			
Appropriate response when sharing request is denied			
Honors sharing requests appropriately			
Denies sharing requests appropriately			

Notes:

Appendix B: Individualized Education Program Goals

Individualized Education Program Goals

The Individualized Education Program (IEP) is a document that defines the individualized objectives of a child who has been determined to have a disability that will impact their ability to receive an appropriate public education. Each IEP is tailored to meet the individual students' needs, as determined by evaluation (assessments and evaluations by school psychologists, standardized tests, performance on academic tasks, etc.). To meet those needs, the IEP includes measurable annual goals addressing each area of need.

As you have learned through these materials, sharing is a complex social skill that involves knowing what can and can't be shared, how to appropriately ask to share, giving appropriate responses when peers ask to share, and displaying appropriate responses when a peer responds to (honors or denies) a sharing request. In addition, there are many different categories of things that can be shared, such as information and suggestions, toys and play equipment, and supplies.

Below are several suggested sharing goals. A good goal is one that is individualized for the student, reflects the student's current level of performance, and is a reasonable expectation for improvement over the course of the IEP year.

Sample Sharing Goal #1:
During unstructured play, will share with 1 – 2 peers for _____ minutes with no more than _____ adult prompt(s) in ___ out of ___ opportunities for _____ consecutive days, as measured by teacher/staff data and observation.

Sample Sharing Goal #2:
During unstructured play, will share with 1 – 2 peers with no problem behaviors in _____ out of _____ opportunities for _____ consecutive days, as measured by teacher/staff data and observation.

Sample Sharing Goal #3:
During group activities, will share materials/allow peers to share suggestions on _____ out of _____ opportunities for _____ consecutive days, as measured by teacher/staff data and observation.

Notes:

Appendix C: For the ABA Professional

Sharing

Use the materials in this book as a part of a comprehensive approach to teaching appropriate flexibility skills.

Purpose and Goal: The **purpose** of this program is to increase sharing in social situations.
The **goal** is to increase identification of appropriate sharing situations and strategies via role play scenarios.

Procedure:

The following are potential behaviors and goals. Successfully implemented Applied Behavior Analysis (ABA) therapy is individualized; specific behaviors and goals should be determined for each student. Remember, goals should be clear, concise, and easy to objectively track.

1. Define **behaviors** for each learner (use the data sheet on the following page). Examples (will vary on a learner by learner basis):
    a. "Identification of sharing situation" is defined as independently identifying whether it is appropriate or inappropriate to share a given item or activity.
    b. Tantrum behavior is defined as hitting, kicking, screaming, or eloping when asked to share.
2. Define **goals** for each learner for each behavior (use the data sheet on the following page). Examples:
    a. Sharing: Student A will suggest a minimum of 2 solutions to a sharing scenario as defined in the target.
    b. Tantrum: Student A will exhibit 0 tantrum episodes across 3 consecutive social scenarios for a given target.
3. Determine **targets** for each learner (use data sheet on the following page).
    a. Reduce the skill/behavior into smaller elements.
4. Use appropriate ABA procedures, such as prompts and prompt fading, errorless teaching, etc., to teach individual elements.
5. Use reinforcement to strengthen each new element.
6. Continue presenting opportunities until the learner(s) have mastered the goal at that target. We recommend continuing a target until the learner responds correctly on at least 80% of the opportunities for several consecutive sessions.
7. Use the suggested activities below to contrive opportunities to work on the targets.

> **Preferred Activity** – Provide your students with an environment that includes several neutral or less preferred activities/toys and one activity/toy that is highly preferred for all students within the group. Tell the students that no one may use the highly preferred activity/toy for the entire play period and that if the activity/item presents a problem amongst the group, it will be removed from the area.
>
> **Discrimination Activity** – Give your students an assignment in which they must construct an "All about me" poster. In the instructions, list several examples of personal information that may include on their poster. Make sure that within this list there are many examples of personal information that can be shared, and a few examples of personal information that should not be shared. However, do not sort the examples into these categories for the students. Once their poster is finished, review with each student any personal information included on the poster that should not be shared. If non-shareable information is included, have them re-do the poster without that information included. Once all students' posters include only shareable information, have them share their poster with the rest of the group.
>
> **Work Activity** – Provide your students with a work activity that requires a specific item to accomplish the activity (task- harder math & item- calculator, task- paint a flower & item- paint brush, etc.). After presenting the work, give the students fewer of the required items than there are students within the group (three students and two calculators, two students and one paint brush, etc.). To make the task more difficult for more advanced learners, give a time limit to the task.

Student: _____

Behavioral Definitions and Goal(s):

Behavior	Definition	Goal

Target	Date Target Introduced	Date Target Mastered

About The Authors

Carl Dzyak, M.Ed. (Special Education, George Mason University), BCBA, LBA is the founder and CEO of Green Box ABA. He founded Green Box ABA, PLLC in October 2014. Carl has been a practicing behavior analyst since 2011 and has worked with individuals on the autism spectrum since 2007.

Barbara Kaminski, Ph.D (Psychology/Behavior Analysis, West Virginia University), BCBA-D, LBA is the ABA Clinical Director at Green Box ABA, PLLC. She teaches graduate level courses in ABA for both George Mason University and The Chicago School of Professional Psychology and maintains an Adjunct Faculty appointment at The Johns Hopkins University School of Medicine Department of Psychiatry and Behavioral Sciences. Dr. Kaminski has been working in clinical practice since 2013 and in the broader field of behavior analysis for over 20 years.

Chris Richardson, M.Ed. (Special Education, George Mason University), BCBA, LBA is COO of Green Box ABA, PLLC. He has been working in Applied Behavior Analysis since 2012 and has worked with children with special needs since 2007.

About The Artist

Sarah Miller began her art career with Game Design and Animation studies at The Art Institute of Washington, and later ended at George Mason University where she earned her Bachelor's of Individualized Study in Visual Arts and Narrative. She is a digital artist and game designer with a passion for creating, no matter its medium —there is nothing she loves more than bringing characters and worlds to life, "bridging connections between people with art and inspiration."

About Green Box ABA, PLLC

Green Box ABA, PLLC is an Applied Behavior Analysis (ABA) clinic located in Springfield, Virginia that provides innovative Applied Behavior Analysis therapy and high quality resources to clients seeking meaningful behavioral change. The therapy is rooted in science, but the approach is rooted in compassion.

www.ingramcontent.com/pod-product-compliance
Lightning Source LLC
Chambersburg PA
CBHW042032150426
43200CB00002B/22